T0064679

UNCONVENTIONAL MEANS

UNCONVENTIONAL MEANS

Building and Re-Building in Small to Medium Chunks

MATT JENSEN

Archway Publishing books may be ordered through booksellers or by contacting:

Archway Publishing
1663 Liberty Drive
Bloomington, IN 47403
www.archwaypublishing.com
1 (888) 242-5904

ISBN: 978-1-4808-2788-2 (sc)
ISBN: 978-1-4808-2789-9 (e)

Library of Congress Control Number: 2016902895

Print information available on the last page.

Archway Publishing rev. date: 03/04/2016

THE INTRODUCTION

Hi! My name is Matt Jensen, and I very much appreciate you picking up my little book! So thanks for that, and for letting me tell you a story that has so many versions, it is more than likely you have heard one.

The Story:

About six months ago Michelle came home to BBQ beef ribs that I managed to get just right. Being the carnivore she is, the melting in your mouth, falling off the bone, squishing and oozing, succulent-sauce-covered-infused-and-encrusted beef ribs looked and smelled like the start of a terrific evening. But her cry of **"Yummy!"** did not ring with that certain playful delightedness with which I was familiar. Something was wrong.

It was **"News from Big Corp."** **Big Corp.** would soon cease to exist. Eight years of salary backing into retirement. Health Plan. Life Insurance. Gym Membership. Various and assorted benefits that filter down to faithful employees. Gone. All Gone. There will be some pension for her thirty-five years of being outstanding in her work for **Big Corp.** But much smaller than it was supposed to be.

There is a very high probability that at this moment you saying to yourself *Yep. I've heard a version of this story.*

I sat motionless in my favorite chair. When I was finally able to respond I quickly sprang into action by mumbling "Now what?" for three days while walking around in a circle. The kitchen flooring needs to be replaced so the new circular trench is not as damaging to our interests as it might otherwise have been. I am now calm. Michelle is one of **"The Faithful Seven"** who will be there to the very end of **Big Corp.** It's really putting a hurt on her.

Many of you understand this context in which many days of prayer, number crunching, worst case - best case projecting, options assessment, etc. etc. continue. Our situation is serious—but not catastrophic as it has been for so, so many. But **Deadly Serious nonetheless.**

Fortunately, the greatest part of this book is not just a story about our **"News from Big Corp." "News from Big Corp."** is a phrase which from this point on will refer to any form of serious financial reversal. This book is for anyone who has received **News from Big Corp.**, for anyone who wants to prepare against **News from Big Corp.**, and for anyone who wants to help a friend or family member who has received **News from Big Corp.**

But before we can go any further you must know three things:

1.   This book **will not** help you or anyone else get a new salary or job—**at least not directly.**

2.   This book **will** help you and anyone else who thinks it's always great to save and make small to medium chunks of money. If you don't think this way, and have received **News from Big Corp.**, please start now! Please proceed to #3.

3.   This book **will** help you and anyone else who likes to negotiate, "do deals", and is open to new ways of saving and making small to medium chunks of money.

What follows is a mishmash of stories, opportunities and techniques. It is an incomplete account of the "who, what, when, where and whys" of how, over the years, Michelle and I have saved and made a great deal of money in small to medium chunks. I hope to have further great successes using what you'll find below, and I hope you will join me as you build, rebuild, and/or assist someone else.

The rest of the introduction followed by the rest of the book:

I am a 54 year old "flying-by-the-seat-of-my-pants" non-traditionally employed, buying, selling, trading, bartering, painting, Intellectual Property Consulting Guy. It's a long story.

Our **News from Big Corp.** means that I must find and maintain a "higher gear." I will need to find and maintain it regardless of whether or not Michelle gets "plugged back in."

Plant closures, lay-offs, jobs lost to China, bankruptcies (the case with **Big. Corp.**), etc. I thought it would be a "Phenomenal Thing" if I could actually help a very large number of folks with what had worked - and continues to work for us.

The "Risk-Reward Ratio" as represented in Archway's contract made me believe I could write a small little book naming specific places you can go and get a deal on things you need, **by using simple techniques made powerful by words anyone can understand and use**. In this—my little book— **you will not find** any complicated formulas to follow, any fancy banking and/or financial balancing acts to maintain, any schemes that make you dependent on others, and/or any counsel on investments other than **"You need to spend $5.00 and buy my book."** Michelle and I want to say **"Thanks!"** for the little royalty we'll get from your purchase. **You'll get much more!**

If you find any mistakess—no doubt of many types—just blame me for them as I did my own editing in order to save money. I definitely would have paid for editing had the money been there. I know you understand and will forgive me. In terms of nice people to work with ... I asked for and received a 20% discount from Archway when I signed up. They responded to our **News from Big Corp.**—as have so many other nice people!

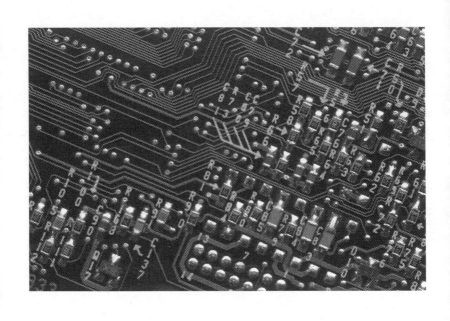

CHAPTER ONE: THE ESSENTIALS

The next sentence expresses one of the top essentials—but it is not at the top.

Deals are lost through procrastination! At some point many of the large mothership companies will change policies and eliminate some of the opportunities presented here. And then there's all those other deals you could have had or done if you had not put them off.

Everything depends on the next sentence!

You must speak directly to the person who has the power to say "YES".

Situation: You are trying to get a deal at a place that has multiple levels of management (this includes husbands and wives). **You must understand** that if someone speaks on your behalf to **the person who has the power to say "Yes"**, the answer is much, much more likely to be **"No."** It is much more likely to be **"No"** because It is incredibly easy for **the person who has the power to say "Yes"** to say **"No"** to the person speaking on your behalf, as opposed to saying it to your face.

If you must speak to a person who does **not** have the power to say **"Yes"**, make sure they understand that you would like to speak face-to-face with **the person who has the power to say "Yes." "Would you please ask the manager (VP, Owner, etc.)**

to come up (down, over, whatever) and see me?" I have done deals over the phone so do not shy away if a non-face-to-face-communication is the only avenue open to speaking with **the person who has the power to say "Yes."**

The Same Situation Once Again: You are trying to get a deal where there are multiple levels of management and you do not know **the person who has the power to say "Yes."** Unless obvious, or until proven otherwise, **you must presume you are speaking with the person who has the power to say "Yes."**

If the person with whom you are speaking **is the person who has the power to say "Yes",** they will feel insulted if you say something like **"Could you direct me to the manager (owner, VP, etc.)?"**

But if you say: **"Hello. I was wondering if you are the manager (or owner, VP, etc.) because I wanted to ask about ..."** and they just so happen to be **the person who has the power to say "Yes",** they will feel complimented because you recognized their "aura of authority." If they are not **the person who has the power to say "Yes",** they will still feel complimented because you recognized their "aura of authority." If they are not **the person who has the power to say "Yes"** you will have built a bridge to them that will stand up nicely if they should become **the person who has the power to say "Yes",** or are given that authority when the manager, owner, VP, etc. is on vacation, sick, etc.

The Rest of the Essentials:

- **Educate yourself.** Acquire price guides, "Buy and Sell" magazines, and information guides on all sorts of "stuff." I pulled into a drive three hours after the yard sale was over and asked the man if I could look around. **"Help yourself—but there's nothing left"**, he said. I walked through and found a rather strange looking antique tie hanger in a closet. He asked for $.50. I sold it for $10.00. The moral of the story? **There is a collector for almost everything.**

- If you have a vehicle (especially a minivan), inside and outside storage capacity, a freezer, and many forms of payment options: cash, debit, cheque, credit card(s), and/or line of credit, you are in an optimum position to make the most of this book.

- **You will not get every deal.** People will say **"No."** Stop negotiating when it is obvious that the **"No"** is final. **Becoming visibly upset is never okay.** Becoming visibly upset will "burn bridges" that will be very difficult to rebuild.

- **If you do not ask you will not get.** How do you know that Mr. Farmer won't sell that lovely heap of foundation stones for next to nothing? That lovely heap of foundation stones that will build a beautiful little wall on your property and hence make it more attractive on the market. If you have received **News from Big Corp.** you know that you might need to sell.

- **Half a pie is better than no pie at all.**

- **Be honest and treat people with respect.**

- **Good ideas are where you find them.** Good ideas and information come from an amazing amount of sources: bulletin boards, magazines at the doctor's office, signs on roads, your Mom's bridge club, the people speaking too loudly in the next booth, the

TV, online, friends, acquaintances, government announcements, etc., etc.

- Using a generic term like "stuff" tends to lower "the esteem", and hence the value of those items in the mind of the seller. The term does not work with items are of a very high quality and/or "big-ticket" items.

CHAPTER TWO: THE SCROUNGE

The Scrounge refers to a mode of existence in which your eyes and ears are constantly scanning your landscape **(the people with whom you speak, the places you visit, the roads on which you travel, the media forms you ingest: TV, books, magazines, newspapers)** for information, opportunities and items that will result in saving and/or making money. You want

- connections for employment
- usable and valuable free stuff
- stuff to sell, trade, and barter
- ideas to sell
- etc.

Who knows what idea, ad for a job, photo contest info, company to call, etc. may come out of the magazine you pick up at the doctor's office? **The Scrounge** is a very rewarding mode of existence. You will learn new things, gain self-confidence, pay your bills, make new friends, strengthen relationships, and have some great times.

Be prepared to seize any and all opportunities by always keeping the following in your vehicle and/or on your person (as applicable):

- Business cards.

- A short handled round-mouth shovel. A high quality collapsible one is usually best.

- A tape measure.

- A large plastic rectangular storage bin for trees, plants, etc.

- One of those new-fangled electronic devices that will do anything for you. Pictures are always great as there are many, many photo contests.

- A notebook or some other means to record opportunities. The new-fangled device no doubt.

- Your chequebook, cash, CCs.

- Garbage bags.

- Clean containers for wild food.

- A wild food/mushroom book.

- A hand saw, box cutter, hammer, wrenches, wire cutters, screwdrivers.

- Maps. Maps? With a map you can use little dots with a legend to remember opportunities. Yes I know I am living in the past. There is probably an app for that. GPS if you like. I still like maps. They are colorful!!

- Water jugs for spring water.

- Binoculars.

NO.

CHAPTER THREE: YOU GET A "NO"

NEVER burn a bridge! Not everyone will say **"Yes."** Many will say **"No."** Many will say **"No"** now but later they may say **"Yes."**

When I ask for a deal and get an unqualified **"No"** I immediately say in an upbeat and friendly tone **"Well I really appreciate it all the same so thanks!"** When receiving a **"No"** that is a definite **"No"** you must end on a high note. You must practise this because ending a sentence with a low and/or dropping off tone communicates disappointment or worse.

<u>**You must NEVER show disappointment, regret, anger or any other negative emotion when someone says "No."**</u> If you react negatively you are creating stress and hard feelings that will make people reluctant to deal with you. If you go away happy after receiving a **"No"**, the next time **the person who has the power to say "Yes"** sees you they will be more prone to think *He was nice about being turned down last time so I will give this guy a break if I can.* Practice your response to receiving a **"No"** because there are places to which you will return.

Any attempt to negotiate after a firm and clear "No" is communicated will severely damage the prospect of future opportunities at that venue. Take people at their word and treat them with respect.

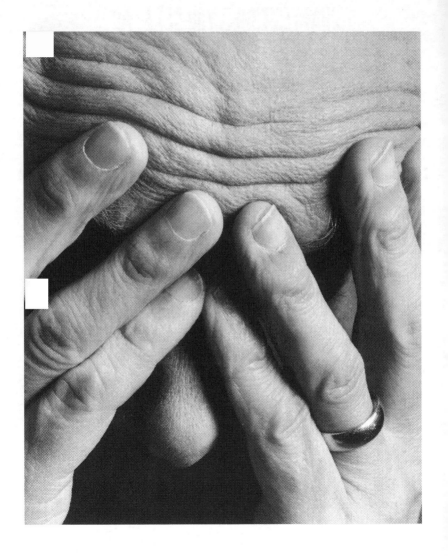

CHAPTER FOUR: THE SOB STORY CLOSE

The Sob Story Close is your account of your **News from Big Corp.,** and it is absolutely **HUGE!** It took me about .001 of a second to get over the embarrassment of getting a deal by telling our **News from Big Corp.** Remember that we are discussing your future, and your family's future. We are discussing whether or not you lose your house, whether or not you have medical benefits, whether or not you have money for your kids' education, etc., etc., etc. So please get over whatever embarrassment you have in using **The Sob Story Close,** and get on with rebuilding your life!

A very high percentage of people have received **News from Big Corp.,** are related to someone who has received **News from Big. Corp.,** and/or know someone who has received **News from Big Corp.** Because of this, the vast majority of people **will not** think less of you because you used **The Sob Story Close.** They will in fact respect you because they will see that you understand the seriousness of your situation, and are willing to put aside your pride for your own sake, and for the sake of your family.

Most people understand and are willing to help if they can. And most want to help—if they can.

You can use **The Sob Story Close** anywhere that deals in any situation where you can achieve a savings of $25.00 + on a single item, more than $25.00 on several items, and on non-consumable items. This includes your mechanic, dentist, chiropractor, vet, etc. You **are not** going to use it to save $10.00 on 4 boxes of cereal.

Two warnings about the Sob Story Close:

1. **The Sob Story Close has a limited life span!** You may appropriately use **the Sob Story Close** within a year of the **news from Big Corp.'s** "critical impact." The date of the last paycheck is more than appropriate. I have been using **the Sob Story Close** since word of **Big Corp.'s** bankruptcy hit the papers. Use **the Sob Story Close** beyond the one year date and most people will think that you should be well into your rebuilding phase, and hence you are inappropriately "milking it." And they would be right!

2. **Do I really need to tell anyone how disgusting and damaging it would be to create and use a "fake News from Big Corp. story?"**

When trying to get a deal using **The Sob Story Close** I have used one of two methods:

1. **The Straight Ask Close.**

In **The Straight Ask Close** you are simply going straight in for a deal. For the seller the choice is **"Yes"** or **"No."**

Tires for instance:

"You probably heard about what happened to Big Corp. After thirty-five years with Big Corp. my wife is losing 8 years of salary heading into our retirement, all our health benefits, insurance, the vast majority of her pension etc. So we are

rebuilding. Is there anything you can do to help by knocking a few bucks off the tires? " Note: You can be specific with a number and I do recommend it.

Or

2. **The Option Close. Tires again:**

"You probably heard about what happened to Big Corp. After thirty-five years with Big Corp. my wife is losing 8 years of salary heading into our retirement, all our health benefits, insurance, the vast majority of her pension etc. So we are rebuilding. Is there anything you can do to help by knocking $60 off the tires or by throwing in the install?"

Please notice three things about The Option Close:

1. You are creating in the person's mind a choice between **"Yes I will give you a deal on the tires"** or **"Yes I will throw in the install."** Yes or Yes. The choice is not as it is with **The Straight Ask Close: "Yes I will give you a deal on the tires."** or **"No I cannot give you a deal on the tires."** Yes or No.

2. Let us say that in this situation you believe that the car shop guy will be reluctant to give you a deal on the tires, but is more open to giving you a deal on the install. You can increase your chances by making the difference in the savings a little larger than it might be—but not too much. This will help him because by widening the cap a little the lesser deal becomes much easier to give. If you ask for $70 off the tires rather than $60: **"Is there anything you can do to help by knocking $70 off the tires or by throwing in the install?"** you are pushing him into thinking *I can't do*

$70 on the tires—that's too much. But I can throw in the install.

People want to give a deal if they can. In **The Option Close** the choice is between **"Yes"** and **"Yes."** Of course they may still say **"No."** Help them give you the deal they want to give. It can certainly be argued that in the right hands **The Option Close** is the more successful close, but remember that ...

3. If you are trying to get a deal on a "big ticket" item like tires, you might want to use **The Straight Ask Close** rather than **The Option Close**. If they say **"Yes"** on tires when you use **The Straight Ask Close,** your deal will be greater because a free install is less of a deal to you than the $60 (or $70 or $80 or more) deal on the tires.

Here is a variant on **The Option Close** in that the value of the items in question, and the value of the optional deals is quite close:

"I like both the Coopers and the Good-Years. The Coopers would work for me at $320 as opposed to $370 and the Good-years at $340 as opposed to $400."

Please Note: Like many of the techniques to follow, **The Straight Ask Close** and **The Option Close** can be used whether or not there has been **News from Big Corp.**

Please Note: You can ask for a deal even if the item in question is already on sale. This will become clearer in **Chapter Eleven: The Grocery Store.**

CHAPTER FIVE: THE THING YOU DRIVE

Because you are now operating according to **The Scrounge**, your vehicle has become a working entity. **Whenever, wherever, and for whatever reason the vehicle is in motion, the goal must be to have it pay for itself and more!** Whenever your vehicle moves you need to be **safely** scanning for opportunities, making notes, going to a job, and/or picking up goods to sell, trade, barter or use. You must be able to haul stuff of all sorts.

Let me give you an example. I go to another town for my physiotherapy. When in that town I always go to the local grocery stores to see if I can get a deal. I am already there so I try and make the trip (the car and my time) pay for itself in this and other ways. There is also a university in that town that sells books I can resell, and the town is famous for having a lot of hewn stone foundations and walls. Foundation stones are quite useful and hence valuable so I always look around for some. We are in the winter season so at the moment **The Scrounge** for stones is proving quite challenging. Other opportunities are waiting!

A minivan is the best vehicle to have. If you do not have a vehicle that can haul stuff starting thinking about how to get one.

Be prepared to seize any and all opportunities by always keeping the following in your vehicle:

- Business cards.

- A short handled round mouth shovel. A high quality collapsible one is usually best.

- A tape measure.

- A large plastic rectangular storage bin for collected stuff or dirt for trees, plants, etc.

- One of those new-fangled electronic devices that will do anything for you. Pictures are always great as there are many, many photo contests.

- A notebook or some other means to record opportunities. The new-fangled electronic devise no doubt.

- Your chequebook, cash, CCs.

- Garbage bags.

- Clean containers for wild food.

- A Wild food/mushroom book.

- A Hand saw, box cutter, hammer, wrenches.

- Maps. Maps? With a map you can use little dots with a legend to remember opportunities. Yes I know I am living in the past. There is probably an app for that. GPS if you like. I still like maps. They are colorful!

- Water jugs to acquire spring water.

- Binoculars.

Your vehicle must be used efficiently:

- Always try to make your vehicle move in a circuit: POINT A to POINT B to POINT C to Point D ... eventually back to POINT A or wherever you want to be without unnecessarily back-tracking over the same old ground. Plan to do as many chores and chase as many opportunities at one time as you can.

- At all times possible drive at a speed lower than the speed limit. I do a lot of highway driving and I estimate that since slowing down I have saved 15% on my gas bill. **Why was I speeding?** Speeding increases the wear and tear on your vehicle, costs more money in gas, and increases the risk of loss in the form of speeding tickets, an accident, and a rise in insurance costs. **Stop being stupid like I was being—stop speeding right now!**

- **Gas.** We have a credit card that gives us 4% back on gas purchases. Combine that with the discount given where we usually get gas and it adds up nicely. Check and see on what day of the week gas prices are adjusted and you can save in this way as well. Find a no fee free credit card that gives you a good percentage back on your gas purchases.

- **Weight.** Snow on your vehicle and stuff inside the vehicle costs you money in gas and in wear and tear on your vehicle. The other day I picked up some books I knew I could sell. There were 14 boxes weighting approx. 350 pounds. When I arrived home I was tired but that did not matter. The vehicle was going to move the next day and 350 extra pounds of books in the vehicle would cost money. So I carried all the boxes into the house before Michelle and I sat down to supper.

- Remember to record your mileage so you can "write it off" if possible.

Your vehicle's maintenance:

- **Why are you buying new parts for an older vehicle?** You can save a ton on parts buying them from auto salvage places.

- **Synthetic oil.** I use it and I cannot say for certain that I am getting better gas mileage. The oil change costs twice as much but the amount of oil changes are cut in half, so I am spending less time getting my vehicle serviced. So I save a little time, a little mileage and as the oil is better my vehicle will—all other things being equal—last longer.

- **Your mechanic.** Our vehicle had 150,000 miles on it and was due for some major work. I told my down-to-earth, small-shop, honest mechanic/owner about our **News from Big Corp. (The Sob Story Close)** and he knocked $225.00 off the bill! The week before he had arrived home after working away from home for four months. He understood. After I paid he led me out back to his high bush U-Pick blueberry bushes and let me fill a few containers for free. **What a great guy!** But I already knew that.

- **Negotiate.** Negotiate on tires, parts, and service.

CHAPTER SIX: CREDIT CARDS

We use credit cards because so far we have been able to pay them off without incurring their hefty penalties. We have a personal line of credit on our house with a significantly lower interest rate than the cards. The amount we save on food using my techniques easily outstrips the cost of using the line of credit to pay off the cards. **If you are able to pay the CCs off or use a line of credit with a low interest rate there are HUGE opportunities out there. Make sure the card has no fees or hidden costs.**

- **We use a card which gives us 4% back on gas and 2% on everything else.**

- Here is a nice example of what can be done with cards: We signed up for **two** cards that offered a one-time bonus of **20,000 air miles per card for $500.00 worth of purchases**. **The air miles were worth $200.00 in groceries** at a grocery chain that has more than one location close by. After we had spent $500.00 per card on necessary items, we paid off the cards using the line of credit, cancelled them, and redeemed our points for $400 in groceries! **The return was just under 40%!** What a deal!

- By using a credit card in combination with a freezer you can score big at the grocery store! More on this later.

Free

CHAPTER SEVEN: FREE STUFF

Free trees. As you move about you will notice land for sale. If the land in question is slated for development—perfect! Contact the owner or appropriate person in charge and say **"I noticed your parcel of land will be developed so I was wondering if it would it be okay for me to take some foot high oaks, maples, beeches, chestnuts etc. off it before they are gone?"** You can sell them through free local online ads, at a farmer's market, and/or garage sale for $5 - $7 per tree or more. Or you can enhance your own property and its value by using them. We have a very private property on which many scrounged trees are growing quite nicely!

<u>Remember:</u> **When sourcing trees to sell and/or for landscaping, you might find fruit trees and wild food such as mushrooms and berries.**

Free Wild Food. In my little corner of the world we have a large amount of government owned land, and a large number of old abandoned farms on which wild food grows. So if you see a big old apple tree full of apples on an old abandoned farm, ask the guy next door about it. Chances are you are "good to go", but always make the effort to ensure you have permission. **The same applies to blueberries, strawberries, rosehips, mushrooms, fiddleheads, etc.**

In many cases folks do not pick the wild food on their property. **If you nail down any source for free wild food make sure you**

give the folks a goodly amount if for no other reason than to say "Thanks." Chances are you will nail down the source for years. This past summer Michelle and I scored 50 pounds of wild blueberries on an old farm that has never used pesticides and herbicides. The berries are fantastic and the 50 pounds represent a year's worth of blueberry deserts. We could have picked more if my tried old back had allowed it. Feeling better now thanks. Next year we'll be back!

Remember: Genuine gratitude for a good score naturally leads to more!

Free Cultivated Food. One day Michelle and I noticed a sign at the end of a long driveway: **"Vegetables and Greenhouse Plants for Sale."** We went up the long drive to a rather laid-back looking hobby farm compound. After some introductions and a bit of pleasant conversation I told the farmer about our **News from Big Corp.,** and asked if he needed any help as we were willing to work for food. **Are you willing?** Our hour of work netted us a new friendship, lots of fresh air and exercise in a beautiful place, 10 pounds of potatoes, a big bag of carrots, some corn on the cob (all grown without herbicides and pesticides), a beautiful 5 pound roast of beef, great tips for our own little garden, the right to glean his woods for mushrooms, and a chance to pick up a few bucks doing some painting.

Dirt Cheap High Quality Lumber. Three years ago now I came across a little private sawmill while running some errands. I pulled in and asked the mill owner if he had any odd bits of this and that left over from unfilled orders, odd orders, etc. Almost every small sawmill owner has a conglomeration of pieces in storage: 6 of that, 8 of those—you get the picture. I scored superior cedar lumber at a fraction of the cost of what I would have paid for inferior material, and greatly enhanced our property with it!

It gets better. This gentleman's home/hobby farm/woodlot/ sawmill compound has a spring from which he waters his horses. So I said **"Would you mind if I came by once in a while and filled a few jugs with water from your spring?"** **"No problem—help yourselves"**, he said. And so we scored an ongoing source of free, fresh, clean, non-chemically-treated water. May I ask how much do you pay for water, and if it is any good?

<u>Remember</u>: Observe and ask.

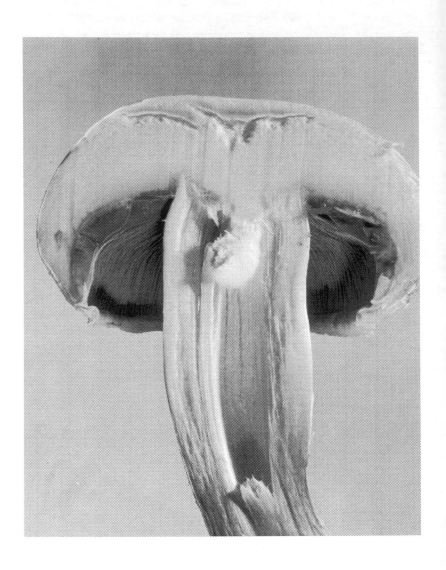

CHAPTER EIGHT: YOUR MUSHROOM FARM

Do you have a piece of ground with a small patch of forest? Here you go:

> http://mycosource.com/mushroom-growing-in-new-brunswick/

CHAPTER NINE: THE FARMER'S MARKET

Your **farmer's market** is a place where you can meet friends new and old, gather valuable info, make new contacts, and of course ... generate revenue—if it is large enough of course. Think of those scrounged trees, that wild food, and your handsomely crafted products made from scrounged items of stone, wood and metal. Perhaps you will license a sauce as I am currently trying to do?

Your **farmer's market** is also a place where you can get gourmet/specialty food at a great price! At the time of closing many vendors will have unsold food. Here is your chance to cut a deal: **"I noticed that you have about 10 bowls of clam chowder left. If I bought what remained would you give me a price of...?"**

CHAPTER TEN: BEER

Of course beer deserves its own chapter.

I started brewing my own beer and it was easy! Each week I drink six or seven good quality pints—usually during football games. Brewing my own beer and drinking approximately the same amount saves us hundreds of dollars each year! I cannot tell you exactly how much as beer consumption may fluctuate—as we all know. Why didn't I start doing this earlier? Because I believed it was not possible for me to brew a beer that I would fully enjoy. **I was wrong!**

- Brewing your own beer only works if you do not cut corners. Use good equipment and buy a good quality kit with the proper beer enhancers. "Dry Hopping" is the way to go!

- Have someone that is grounded in the art help you with your first kit.

- Bottles that have the porcelain/rubber/metal device stoppers save money because you do not need caps or a capper. One of the brands that uses such a device is Grolsch. If you do not have any of these bottles, pretty much every recycling depot has them put aside for guys and gals like you who have decided to brew their own. The cost is usually $.20 each.

CHAPTER ELEVEN: THE GROCERY STORE

Fasten your seat-belt because this is HUGE!

Most large grocery stores have many layers of management:

- The store's General Manager. This is a person with whom you will probably never speak.
- The manager on duty.
- The meat manager.
- The deli manager.
- The fish department manager.
- The dry goods (grocery) manager.
- The bakery manager.

NEVER EVER "go over the head" of any manager to someone higher up the "food chain." So if the seafood manager is **the person who has the power to say "Yes"** on a seafood deal, do not appeal to the manager on duty if they say **"No."** If they say **"That it is Mr. H. or Ms. G's call."** it's okay to ask for them if the size of the deal warrants it. **Always show respect for someone's authority.**

I arrive at the grocery store. I get a shopping cart and if I have shopped there before ...

1. I get the name of the manager on duty. This is often found on a chart near or at the service desk. If the manager on duty is a person who will not give a deal I immediately

proceed to the deli, seafood, meat, etc. departments. We will get to those departments in a minute.

2. If the manager on duty does give a deal or is someone I do not know ...

   a. I immediately proceed to the place where the store displays goods which have been substantially marked down.

   b. I find an item I like and **if the number is not too large to handle I take all of them. This is key!** If you are willing to take all of a particular item that is marked down, you will probably remove that "sku" from the database and make the manager's life easier.

   c. I then look to see if there is a strong "secondary" choice and I take all or some of them. This will be explained below.

   d. I roll up to the service desk and in a firm, polite and friendly way ask for the manager to come to the service desk (or wherever) and speak with me. **Do you remember Chapter #1? That upon which everything else depends?** Sure you do!

The manager comes up and I say **"Hi Ms. .... Thanks for coming up to speak with me. I see that you have 15 of "X" at 50% off from $6.00 to $3.00. I would be willing to take all of them at $1.85 and get them out of your system if that works for you."**

If she/he says **"Yes"** then be sure to say **"Thanks a lot I really appreciate it."** If the answer is a clear **"No"**—she/he makes it clear by their response that they cannot or will not move on price—your reply will be to buy them anyway or say **"Well I really appreciate it anyways so thanks."** Always respond in an upbeat tone. If their response is not a clear **"No"** negotiation can take place.

Using the example above, if he/she responds with $2.00 as a counter I will respond by agreeing or countering if I have 1 item but several numbers of it: 10 boxes of the same cereal for instance. If I have "primary" and "secondary" items I will respond with **"I still like my price better but I would also take six (or 7 or whatever) of "x" (the secondary item) at $1.25 as opposed to $1.75 if that works for you."** Now he/she has to think carefully because you are counter-offering to buy **even more** items if they say **"Yes"** to your first price on the first item. If they say **"No"** they may lose everything. Most of the time he/she will say **"Yes"** unless store policy prohibits it.

I use the following variant if the situation warrants it: "**Hi Ms. .... Thanks for coming up to speak with me. I see that you have 15 of "X" at 50% off from $6.00 to $3.00. I have never had these before but I am willing to take a chance and take all of them at $1.85 to get them out of your system if that works for you**." In expressing that you have never before tried the item you wish to buy (of course you will only do this if true), you are communicating to the manager that your offer is more than a good one because

a.   you are making the manager's life easy by taking a sku out of his/her system, and

b.   you might be stuck with food that you and our family will not eat.

Do you see how reasonable you are? The manager does, and certainly does not want to appear unreasonable by turning you down. In this case the manager is more than likely to give you a deal unless they are an unreasonable person, and/or company policy prohibits any further reduction. **And for the record: I can only think of one instance in which I bought food we did not like.** In that case the loss was small and has been easily offset by all the great deals on food that we acquired in this way. And of course you can use a "secondary" item—if there is one that works for you—when you are trying to get a deal on food you have never tried.

This close, with a "primary" and "secondary" item, is a variant of **The Option Close** we saw earlier. A variant **but also different in another way** because in this case the service or product is probably **far less important to you as it may not even be on your list of necessary food items. You can easily "walk."** Tires and an install you need. So walk if it is not going anywhere. Walk and be gracious with thanks when you do.

If they counter your counter that is as far as it can go! So if you say **"I see that you have 15 of "X" at 50% off from $6.00 to $3.00. I would be willing to take all of them at $1.85 to get them out of your system if that works for you."** and they counter with $2.50, **you can counter the $2.25 but you cannot go further than this. They agree with your counter or not and that is it! You accept or not. Remember** that we are talking about groceries, and the manager will not be amused if you drag the thing out and take up his/her time.

Knowing whether the item(s) and its value warrants an extended negotiation is almost as important as your reaction to a **"No."** Unless you are negotiating on groceries worth $150.00, going back and forth beyond your counter-offer to their counter-offer means risking the loss of any possible future deals from the manager with whom you are speaking.

When receiving a **"No"** you must end on a high note. You must practise this because ending a sentence with a low and/or dropping off tone communicates disappointment or worse. **You must NEVER show disappointment, regret, anger or any other negative emotion when someone says "No."** If you react negatively you are creating stress and hard feelings that will make people reluctant to deal with you. If you go away happy after receiving a **"No"**, the next time **the person who has the power to say "Yes"** sees you they will be more prone to think *He was nice about being turned down last time so I will give this guy a break if I can.*

3. I then proceed to the deli, meat, seafood, etc. departments.

The Deli, Seafood and Meat, Bakery Departments. These departments almost always have their own manager: **the person who has the power to say "Yes"**. Almost all items in these departments have a "best before date." On the day of their "best before date" many of these items will receive a direct mark down either first thing in the morning, or before supper in order to get the pre-supper shoppers to "bite down hard." They want them to "bite down hard" because items with a "best before date" are thrown out if not sold before the end of day on their best before date. This results in a 100% loss to the store. If the store closes at 9, or 10, or 11PM try some evening shopping.

In the meat, deli, bakery and seafood departments you will use the same techniques as found in section #2 above.

An alternate approach is to say **"I saw that you had 12 of "X" and I want to leave a few for other customers just in case someone else wants some before closing, … so I would take 8 of them if you could do X"** (the price you are offering). In this approach you are putting into the manager's mind the idea that he will probably **not** sell all of the items that are left before closing in an hour or two, and therefore his loss on whatever is not purchased is **100%**. A few weeks before completing my little book I used this approach and bought five legs of lamb roasts for $10 each. The original price was an average of $40 each!

If a holiday is coming up—like a long weekend—many more items are likely to be thrown out. So check your calendar!

Also, please note that you can combine in one deal two or three or four different items with similar prices: **"I noticed you had three packages of pork-chops for $12.00 each and five packages of boneless chicken breasts at $14.00. If I bought all of these best-before-today-items would you give them to me at 50% off?"** If they say **"They are already marked down."** you can counter with **"Thirty percent rather than 50% would still work for me if it works for you."** or just try a little gentle shrug of your shoulders and wait patiently with a smile.

One thing that is almost always true in negotiating: The person who speaks first loses! So when you counter a counter offer— be patient and wait for them to respond!

Seafood is a tricky thing. It can go bad very quickly and produce very nasty results. Every so often there will be a "major hiccup" and a seafood department will receive seafood it did not order, and/or more than it can handle.

One day I was in the grocery store and noticed one pound frozen blocks of Nova Scotian haddock marked down from $4.00 to $2.00. I picked up a piece, rolled up to the counter, and said **"I noticed the haddock was marked down and was wondering if you had a mega amount delivered by mistake or some other hiccup?"** The manager said **"Let me check out back."** She came back and said **"Well as a matter of fact…"**

As it turned out they had received much more than they could store long term in their walk-in freezer, and what was left was taking up space they needed for more expensive seafood items. The result was a purchase of 144 one pound blocks of Nova Scotian haddock—a $576 value—for $99.00! Go introduce yourself to the seafood manager and say in your own words something like **"I understand that fish is always tricky thing and I was wondering if you had one of those 'hiccups' that sometimes happens, and you've been left with some stuff that you would like to move out asap?"** The next large seafood score could be yours!

IMPORTANT: Using a "generic" term like "stuff" for consumable items lowers the "esteem" of those items in the mind of the person who has the power to say "Yes." By lowering the esteem you lower the value and therefore are more likely to get a deal if there is one to be had.

Remember: Having a freezer or access to one puts you in a much better position to really score big in the meat, deli and seafood departments.

Serious markdowns. This often happens in the deli department—but can also happen in the meat and international food departments. I was scanning through the deli department one day and noticed that one of their specialty cheeses was marked down 65%. When you see this type of markdown it usually means that the manager believes he will be stuck with a load of whatever it is, and take a big "hit." Here is your chance: apply #2 and go crazy. It was in fact a specific deep markdown on a cheese I had never tried that opened my eyes to what could be accomplished at the grocery store. I bought 17 blocks at a price that amounted to 85% off. **Cheese Rocks!**

Share the blessing. As I go through the grocery store I see elderly folks who, by the nature of the goods in their carts, are probably unable to buy high quality food. If you get a great deal ask a senior if they like steak, or fish or whatever. **"Keep it on the Down Low"** to make sure you respect their dignity when you put 1 or 2 or 3 of whatever into their cart. Smile and say "There you go." And then walk away so that their surprise or confusion as to what just happened will not lead to you answering a bunch of questions in earshot of the manager you **DO NOT** want to disturb. It will be good for your soul and more importantly it is the loving thing to do! Be greedy for a deal but not "tight-fisted." **Remember that you may have been hit with News from Big Corp., but you have time and this little tool to help you, whereas they can do very little about the hard circumstances of their old age!**

CHAPTER TWELVE: THE WEB

I have a very small company that sells its product online. One of the domains came up for renewal at $37.99 a year. When I called to renew I told the lady that I was pleased with their service but because of our **News from Big Corp.** (I used **The Sob Story Close**.) I was forced to look at alternatives, and there was one out there at $19.99 per year. The result? She gave me 3 years at $37.99 rather than 1 year at $37.99.

I used **The Sob Story Close** on the webmasters who maintain my site and the result was a permanent 20% reduction is their fees! **Remember: "If you do not ask you will not get."**

I am not very computer literate. Perhaps many of you are thinking *Aha! I know other opportunities in cyber space!*

CHAPTER THIRTEEN: THE PRIORITY CLOSE

The Priority Close is very much like The Sob Story in that it is perfectly legit to use if true, and a perfect example of disgusting dishonesty if applied when not true—OR if used more than once.

In my opinion there are times when a very "legitimate want" clashes against a commitment(s). We had one.

About 9 months before we received our **News from Big Corp.**, we agreed that because watching football represented one of our favourite things to do as a couple, we would look for a new set to replace the ancient 15 year old Toshiba. We also agreed that because we had higher priorities we would only buy a used model (2 years old at most) if it could be purchased at 1/3 of what it was worth new.

I responded to an ad for a 50 inch LG. The gentleman was asking $550 for a set worth $900. I told him upfront **"Michelle and I have the higher priority of ... so we cannot pay more than 1/3 of what a set is worth. I can offer $300 but not a penny more."** A day passed. Another passed. On the third day he called and said he would take the $300. Football never looked better!

Every time you spend a dollar on "X" it means you are not spending that dollar on "Y" or something else. If you are going to lessen the amount you could give away to those less fortunate, because you are buying something that is not an "essential", you are obligated to try and get a deal!

CHAPTER FOURTEEN: FORCE THE ISSUE

In this chapter I will present a couple of additional "Before we received our **News from Big Corp.** items."

The old car was done. At the time I was more in favour of a new car than buying used and found four different vehicles that suited our needs and budget. I phoned all four salesmen and said **"I found four different vehicles that suit our needs and this afternoon I am going to buy from the dealership that gives me the best deal."** I told each what the models were. I could almost hear the salesmen sweat into their phones as each went into why their vehicle was superior. **"I appreciate the features of your vehicle but we will be happy with any of them. It comes down to how much we save. So I will call back in couple of hours."**

I did not try to "shop" each one by saying **"The last guy I spoke with offered X so…."** because I had heard from a reliable source that car salesmen will not respond favourably to such a tactic, and also because it seemed dishonest to do this after structuring the "buying event" as outlined above.

This was nine years ago so I have forgotten the details on price but I can tell you there was a further "meaningful" reduction in price.

I did the same five years when I bought bikes. I said to the owner of the first bike shop I visited: **"I am going to buy**

two bikes today and the shop that gives me the best deal will sell them to me. There are many brands out there which will suit us so it comes down to who is willing and what they are offering." I did not need to go any further because he was willing and I was very happy with what he was offering. I bought a Kona and a Trek—$300 off each.

CHAPTER FIFTEEN: GOING TO THE JOB

Let's say you are going to a job. It is 2 weeks of painting because you are an amateur who can actually do a great job! Terrific! And here is the bonus: For 2 weeks you will go back and forth the same way, or you will experiment with different routes. You now have the opportunity to very thoroughly scan this particular landscape in order to find and seize opportunities. **Think! It's an "amplified" opportunity to scan the landscape because you are going to the job anyway, and you are already writing off the mileage!**

CHAPTER SIXTEEN: FREELANCING

If you are well educated, and/or have marketable experience and skills, there are opportunities for you to "sell yourself."

For instance: **Freelancer.com**

I researched and wrote my own US and Canadian patents for my online company's product. My total cost to get 95% of what I asked for—and within three months of application—was $750. Because of my experience, education and skill I am able to help others who have intellectual property needs—and at a fraction of what they would pay a Patent Agent. They save a tonne and I make some really nice cash!

Michelle has seized the opportunity to freelance and has already completed four separate projects for an internationally operating company based in Germany. Hopefully the German company and others will want her expertise for many, many more projects. The owner sent Michelle some code to work on in order to see if she was any good, and after having received it back he told her that she had **"... exceeded even my expectations."** The point was not that she has exceeded his expectations, it was that she had exceeded **even his** expectations. He considered his standards to be extremely high and she blew him away! Just contact Archway with your info and we'll go from there.

What marketable skills, education and experience do you have?

CHAPTER SEVENTEEN: SELLING YOUR IDEA

You have an idea you think would be great for Company Z. This idea—depending on what it is—**may** fall under one of several Intellectual Property categories such as utility patent, trademark, copyright, or industrial design. You may need to go through the process of protecting what you have. **One thing is certain: you need a non-disclosure contract before you speak with any prospective buyer, or with anyone else to whom you wish to communicate your idea.** That anyone else being someone like me who can help you save a lot of money on patent agent fees. I am not going to go into this too deeply because it would be impossible to do that here. However, here is simple version of a non-disclosure contract:

Nondisclosure Agreement between Mr. Matt Jensen residing at .... and Mr. T.W. residing at ....

The subject of this agreement is a **Toy Idea** developed by Mr. T.W. This agreement includes all material attached to this agreement and designated "Appendix A.: Toy Idea Developed by Mr. T.W." Each page of Appendix A. will be designated by the title "Appendix A.: Mr. T.W.'s Toy Idea Page 1 of...." etc.

The Agreement is as follows:

1.   It is understood that Mr. Matt Jensen is under no obligation to enter into any subsequent contractual agreement(s) with Mr. T.W.

2. It is understood that Mr. T.W. is under no obligation to enter into any subsequent contractual agreement(s) with Mr. Matt Jensen.

3. Mr. Matt Jensen agrees that he will not use, and/or disclose to any third party any information in Appendix A. without the written permission of Mr. T. W. If consultation and hence participation of a third party is required, such approval—and the terms thereof—will be in writing, witnessed, and deemed as part of this agreement.

4. It is understood that this contract is null and void if Mr. T.W.'s idea, as described by Appendix A., already exists in the public domain.

Agreed to by:

Matt Jensen: Date:

Witnessed by:

T.W.   Date:

Witnessed by:

Let us say that your idea needs intellectual property protection and that is in place. Super! You need to contact the company you wish to approach and ask if they will sign a non-disclosure. Please do not have any delusions. The bigger the company, the less likelihood of their speaking with you. Unfortunately more and more companies refuse to look at unsolicited ideas. They have forgotten or never knew that **Good ideas are where you find them.**

You have the protection and you know who you want to contact. **How are you going to do that? Forget sending an email. You must speak to someone on the phone.** How you are going to "break through" to the director of marketing, or the director of new ideas development, or owner, etc. depends on where you are. I live in North America so we will stick to a discussion of the reaction you will most likely get from a company in The US of A., and the reaction you will most likely from a company in Canada.

You must know the differences between the two if you are going to get past the first line of defence: the girl who picks up the phone.

You will say **"Hello. I would like to speak with the new products manager** (or marketing director. etc.). **What is their name please?"** You will ask for the name if you do not know it. You **must** get their name before they answer the phone because starting by a conversation with something like **"Thank you Sir for taking my call. To whom am I speaking please?"** is the "kiss of death!" You should know their name just as you should not presume that someone is **not** the manager. It will be an offense in the same fashion as outlined in **Chapter One: The Essentials.** If the girl transfers you before you get the name, hang up and call back. Apologise for your clumsiness in hanging up and make sure you get that name before once again being transferred!

So let's go back a little. Context: The US of A. **"Hello. I would like to speak with the new products manager please. What is their name?** She gives you the name and you say **"May I speak with him/her please?"** If our gal is in the US of A. she will probably ask **"May I tell him/her your name and what it is about?"** Your response is **"Matt Jensen in …. This is concerning …."** You are through. **Remember:** You are an important person bringing something important, and there is a 50/50 chance that the company and/or director of whatever has not forgotten or insulated itself from the fact that **Good ideas are where you find them.**

Context: Canada. **"Hello. I would like to speak with the new products manager** (or marketing director. etc.). **What is their name please?"** She gives you the name and you say **"May I speak with him/her please?"** In Canada our phone gal will probably ask **"May I tell him/her your name who you are with?"**

Do you see the difference in the two responses?

In the US of A. the phone gal will ask your name, and is very, very likely to ask what the call is about—**not who you are "with"**—because **Americans have the virtue of not caring who you are.** The US of A. is a country of individuals who understand that one person with one idea has real power. They care about the idea or issue. **Who you are "with" is very secondary.** They just want to know what your call is about.

Canada is an oligarchal society.

Oligarchy: a small group of people and/or a small number of small groups having control of a country, organization, or institution.

In Canada you are more likely to be seen as having value, and worth speaking with, if you represent or are a part of some recognised and important institution, whether it be private, public or governmental in nature. If you are not "with someone" she recognises, your stature will drop and there will be a very high probability that she will not let you through. She will stall by telling you he/she is on the phone or out for lunch or something else and then ask for your contact info so he/

she can get back to you. This is very likely to be the response you will get whether or not it is true that they are unavailable. How very poor!

When I call a company or entity in Canada and the phone gal asks **"My I tell them with you are with?** I say in a calm, non-abrasive but firm and commanding tone: **"Matt Jensen in …"** I act and speak as if they should know who I am. This throws our Canadian phone gal off because now she is thinking *I do not know who this person is but Mr. … probably does so I better put him through.* State your name with town or city and state if in the US of A., and town or city with province if in Canada. You do not need to say **"Mr …"** or "**My name is** …" because your name is enough and she **should** know it. **It is a form of bluff but it works very, very consistently.**

Now you are in and the person with whom you want to speak is on the line: **"Ms. … it's Matt Jensen in … thanks for taking my call."** <u>Whether in The US of A., or Canada, you will use the same technique with both the phone gal and the person with whom you want to speak.</u> You want the phone gal to think *I do not know who this person is but Mr. … probably does so I better put him through.,* and you want the person with whom you want to speak—and are now speaking to think *I am not sure who this but this sounds important.* And it is important so sit up in that chair and own it!

This is the **End** and it has been great being with you! I wish you every success and **Remember: It All Adds Up!**

BIO:

My name is Matt Jensen and I am a 54 year old with three Batchelor Degrees. It's a long story. From my father—who was a brilliant engineer (now retired)—I received the ability to be logical and analytical. Michelle would be giggling just a little if she could read this right now. Creativity—including thinking "outside the box"—came from my artistic Mother who was an antique dealer. My sisters and I have been exposed to, and interested in, buying and selling, trading and bartering, and finding "treasure" since we were knee-high to grasshoppers.

I did not have enough "letters after my name" to get the work I wanted, and that, in combination with other factors, including my love of books, led me down the path of being an antiquarian bookseller specializing in academic materials. As an antiquarian bookseller one must find the goods to sell, negotiate a price and then resell said goods. Folks who want information also want the "physical representations" of the information in the books they buy. And so I became a buyer and seller of antiques, books and other tangible goods. Negotiation is in my blood.

In 1999 my love of cycling led to me design and patent a bicycle accessory which I have been selling online for some 16 years. I researched and wrote my own patent and received approval for 95% of what I requested within three months of application. I own Canadian and American patents, several trademarks and a handful of copyrights.

My education, background and extensive knowledge of where I live came together and I became a "flying by the seat of my pants" non-traditionally employed, buying, selling, trading, bartering, intellectual property consulting guy who owns a small one man business.

When **Big Corp.** closes its doors in six weeks we will lose much of our income, all the benefits, and 75%—or more—of Michelle's pension. My knowledge, experience and skills must now became more intensely focused on finding additional ways to save and generate cash. This small book is a direct result of who I am and the situation in which we find ourselves. **I wish you well with my little book!**